rwork stitches

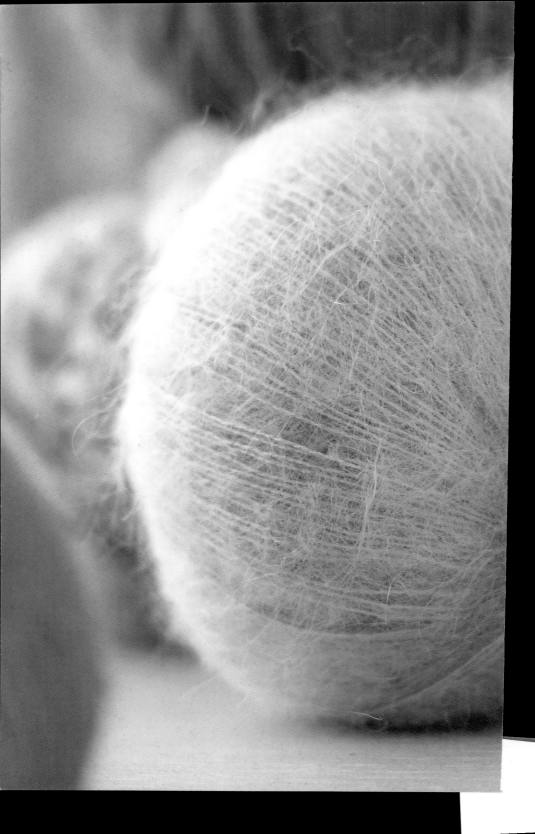

THE HARMONY GUIDES

colourwork stitches

over 250 designs to knit

edited by Susie Johns

COLLINS & BROWN

C&B
CRAFTS

First published in the United Kingdom in 2009 by
Collins & Brown
10 Southcombe Street
London
W14 0RA

An imprint of Anova Books Company Ltd

Picture credits:
2, 5, 7 Michael Wicks
6, 9 top row left and right, second row centre, third row left Corbis
9 third row right, bottom row centre Istock
All other photography by Geoff Dann
Illustrations by Lotte Oldfield

ISBN 978-1-84340-422-4

A CIP catalogue for this book is available from the British Library.

10 9 8 7 6 5 4 3 2 1

Reproduction by Dot Gradations Ltd, UK
Printed and bound by 1010 Printing International Ltd, China

This book can be ordered direct from the publisher.
Contact the marketing department, but try your bookshop first.
www.anovabooks.com

contents

introduction   7

the basics   12

stitch gallery   24

index   270

resources   272

inspiration

Colour is the inspiration for this edition: two or more different coloured yarns cleverly combined to produce a multitude of patterns, each presented as a clear, easy-to follow chart and a knitted stitch sample.

For more than 30 years, The Harmony Guides have provided a unique reference for knitters, providing a wealth of stitch information and inspiration for everyone who likes to knit, regardless of their skill level.

This new generation of Harmony Guides contains not only traditional patterns but new and innovative ones too. Browse through the pages and you will find simple motifs, more intricate patterns and some really challenging designs ready for you to select, combine and incorporate into your knitting projects. Whether you are making a a scarf or hat, jumper or jacket, a cushion cover or a blanket you will find stitch patterns to bring colour and interest into your project.

Fair Isle knitting uses design repeats and motifs in horizontal and vertical bands, and in small and large panels. Typically, Fair Isle patterns feature diagonal lines which means that the colour-change positions are offset, creating an elastic fabric; and no more than two colours are used in any row, one colour being 'stranded' across the back of the other. There is also a symmetry to the patterns, which means they can easily be memorised.

Intarsia knitting is a similar technique, though yarn is usually not stranded across the back of the work and patterns often involve larger blocks of colour and picture motifs.

Most of the designs in this book draw their inspiration from traditional Scottish and Scandinavian patterns and can be combined in all kinds of ways. Traditional Fair Isle designs are usually made up of horizontal bands of patterning. The bands can vary from a single row to 30 or more rows and can be combined with panels and with all-over designs.

Of course, the modern knitter does not have to follow any rules and you can be as creative as you like. A good starting point is to draw your design on graph paper using coloured pencils or pens, or to use a computer program that allows you to create a grid and fill it in with blocks of colour. It also helps to knit swatches, to see how a chosen pattern can change dramatically when various different colour combinations are used, such as changing a background colour from dark to light, by using contrasting or clashing colours or by using different shades and tones of one colour.

Fine yarns are favoured by traditionalists – like me – when knitting Fair Isle patterns. I like to use a two-ply jumper-weight Shetland yarn, combining solid-coloured dyed yarns with natural undyed yarns and with tweedy, flecked yarns for subtle colour changes. These patterns can, however, be knitted using yarns of any weight. The choice is yours.

If the idea of knitting a whole garment in a colour pattern seems too daunting, why not incorporate a patterned border into something that is otherwise plain? You could add a wave border to either end of a scarf, for example, or all round the hem of a knitted skirt or jacket. A jumper or cardigan could feature a Fair Isle band, a patterned medallion on a pocket or a scattering of small motifs. A child's jumper could have a row of Lads and Lasses dancing across the front or a single intarsia motif, while a baby's cradle cover could have flowers or bows all round the edges.

Cushion covers are a blank canvas for all kinds of colourwork. You could add a small colour motif to an otherwise plain panel, large or small; combine a selection of patterns for an all-over design; or save your experimental swatches and tension squares and stitch them all together to make a patchwork.

If you don't have the patience for a big project, think of all the small items you could make using any of the patterns in this book. Knit a single border pattern in your own choice of colours and add elastic to make a headband, a buckle to create a belt or use it as the strap for a shoulder bag. Work patterned strips in the round to make tubes of knitted fabric that can be worn as cuffs or legwarmers or which can be stuffed with wadding to make a funky draught excluder. Stitch two small swatches together and you have a cover for your MP3 player, digital camera or passport or make larger pieces to create a knitted portable computer case.

If you are new to colour knitting and you find you become hooked, pass on your new-found skills to someone else. Then get together with friends or family members and create individual squares that can be joined to make a quilt or picnic blanket – perhaps one that uses every single pattern in the book!

Best of all, be happy in the knowledge that you are helping to continue – and in some cases even revive – a centuries-old knitting tradition.

Susie Johns

tools & equipment

To master any skill, it's imperative to have a solid foundation of the techniques. This section provides useful information that can come in handy while knitting.

Knitting Needles

Knitting needles are used in pairs to produce a flat knitted fabric. They are pointed at one end to form the stitches and have a knob at the other to retain the stitches. They may be made in plastic, wood, steel or alloy and range in size from 2mm to 17mm in diameter. In the UK, needles used to be sized by numbers – the higher the number, the smaller the needle. In the USA, the opposite is true – higher numbers indicate larger sizes. Metric sizing has now been internationally adopted. Needles are also made in different lengths that will comfortably hold the number of stitches required for each project.

It is useful to have a range of sizes available so that tension swatches can be knitted up and compared. Discard any needles that become bent. Points should be fairly sharp; blunt needles reduce the speed and ease of working.

Circular and double-pointed needles are used to produce a tubular fabric or flat rounds. Many traditional fishermen's sweaters are knitted in the round. Double-pointed needles are sold in sets of four or five. Circular needles consist of two needles joined by a flexible length of plastic. The plastic varies in length. Use the shorter lengths for knitting sleeves, neckbands, etc, and the longer lengths for larger pieces such as jumpers and skirts.

Cable needles are short needles used to hold the stitches of a cable to the back or front of the main body of knitting.

Other Useful Equipment

Needle gauges are punched with holes corresponding to the needle sizes and are marked with both the old numerical sizing and the metric sizing so you can easily check the size of any needle.

Stitch holders resemble large safety pins and are used to hold stitches while they are not being worked – for example, around a neckline when the neckband stitches will be picked up and worked after back and front have been joined. As an alternative, thread a larger blunt-pointed sewing needle with a generous length of contrast-coloured yarn, thread it through the stitches to be held while they are still on the needle, then slip the stitches off the needle and knot both ends of the contrast yarn to secure the stitches.

Wool sewing needles or tapestry needles are used to sew completed pieces of knitting together. They are large with a broad eye for easy threading and a blunt point that will slip between the knitted stitches without splitting and fraying the yarn. Do not use the sharp-pointed sewing needles to sew up knitting.

A row counter is used to count the number of rows that have been knitted. It is a cylinder with a numbered dial that is pushed onto the needle and the dial is turned at the completion of each row.

A tape measure is essential for measuring the length and width of completed knitting. For checking tension swatches, it is better to use a rigid ruler. For an accurate result, always smooth the knitting (without stretching) on a firm flat surface before measuring it.

A crochet hook is useful for picking up dropped stitches.

Knitting Yarn

Yarn is the term used for strands of spun fibres that are twisted together into a continuous length of the required thickness. Yarn can be of animal origin (wool, angora, mohair, silk, alpaca), vegetable origin (cotton, linen) or man-made (nylon, acrylic, rayon). Knitting yarn may be made up from a combination of two or more different fibres.

Each single strand of yarn is known as a ply. A number of plys are twisted together to form the yarn. The texture and characteristics of the yarn may be varied by the combination of fibres and by the way in which the yarn is spun. Wool and other natural fibres are often combined with man-made fibres to make a yarn that is more economical and hard-wearing. Wool can also be treated to make it machine washable. If the twist of the yarn is firm and smooth, it knits up into a hard-wearing fabric. Loosely twisted yarn has a softer finish when knitted.

Buying Yarn

Yarn is most commonly sold wound into balls of specific weight measured into grams or ounces. Some yarn, particularly very thick yarn, is also sold in a coiled hank or skein that must be wound into a ball before you can begin knitting.

Yarn manufacturers (called spinners) wrap each ball with a paper band on which is printed a lot of necessary information. The ball band states the weight of the yarn and its composition. It will give instructions for washing and ironing and will state the ideal range of needle sizes to be used with the yarn. The ball band also carries the shade number and dye lot number. It is important that you use yarn of the same dye lot for an entire project. Different dye lots vary subtly and this may not be apparent when you are holding the two balls, but it may show as a variation in shade on the finished piece of knitting.

Always keep the ball band as a reference. The best way is to pin it to the tension swatch (see page 20) and keep them together with any left over yarn and spare buttons or other trimmings. That way you can always check the washing instructions and also have materials for repairs.

the basics

Once you have mastered the basics of knitting, you can go on to develop your skills and start making more challenging projects.

Casting On

1 Make a slip knot 1m (39in) from the end of the yarn. Hold the needle in your right hand with the ball end of the yarn over your index finger. Wind the loose end of the yarn around your left thumb from front to back.

2 Insert the point of the needle under the first strand of yarn on your thumb.

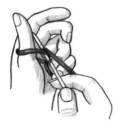

3 With your right index finger, take the ball end of the yarn over the point of the needle.

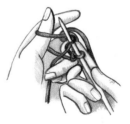

4 Pull a loop through to form the first stitch. Remove your left thumb from the yarn. Pull the loose end to secure the stitch. Repeat until all stitches have been cast on.

Knit Stitch

1 Hold the needle with the cast-on stitches in your left hand, with the loose yarn at the back of the work. Insert the right-hand needle from front to back of the first stitch on the left-hand needle.

2 Wind the yarn from left to right over the point of the right-hand needle.

3 Draw the yarn through the stitch, thus forming a new stitch on the right-hand needle.

4 Slip the original stitch off the left-hand needle, keeping the new stitch on the right-hand needle.

5 To knit a row, repeat steps 1 to 4 until all the stitches have been transferred from the left-hand needle to the right-hand needle. Turn the work, transferring the needle with the stitches to your left hand to work the next row.

Purl Stitch

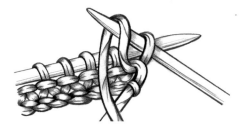

1 Hold the needle with the stitches in your left hand with the loose yarn at the front of the work. Insert the right-hand needle from back to front of the first stitch on the left-hand needle.

2 Wind the yarn from right to left over the point of the right-hand needle.

3 Draw the yarn through the stitch, thus forming a new stitch on the right-hand needle.

4 Slip the original stitch off the left-hand needle, keeping the new stitch on the right-hand needle.

5 To purl a row, repeat steps 1 to 4 until all the stitches have been transferred from the left-hand needle to the right-hand needle. Turn the work, transferring the needle with the stitches to your left hand to work the next row.

Increasing

The simplest method of increasing one stitch is to work into the front and back of the same stitch.

On a knit row, knit into the front of the stitch to be increased, then before slipping it off the needle, place the right-hand needle behind the left-hand needle and knit again into the back of the same stitch. Slip the original stitch off the left-hand needle.

On a purl row, purl into the front of the stitch to be increased, then before slipping it off the needle, purl again into the back of the same stitch. Slip the original stitch off the left-hand needle.

Decreasing

The simplest method of decreasing one stitch is to work two stitches together.

On a knit row, insert the right-hand needle from front to back through two stitches instead of one, then knit them together as one stitch. This is called knit two together (k2tog).

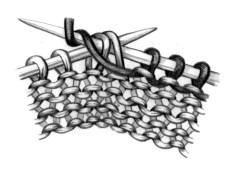

On a purl row, insert the right-hand needle from back to front through two stitches instead of one, then purl them together as one stitch. This is called purl two together (p2tog).

Joining in a new colour on a knit row

When working Fair Isle, it is better to join in a new colour at the beginning of a row, but in some cases, you may have to join in the middle of a row. This is how you join in a new colour mid-row on a knit row.

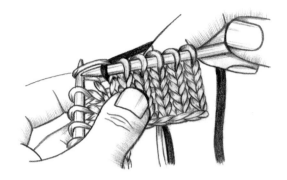

1 Lay the new colour (B) over the original colour (A). Twist the yarns over themselves and hold them in place.

2 Knit with the new colour (B). You can always go back and tighten the join after a couple of stitches.

Joining in a new colour on a purl row

This is how you join in a new colour mid-row on a purl row.

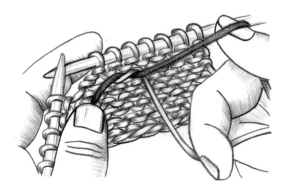

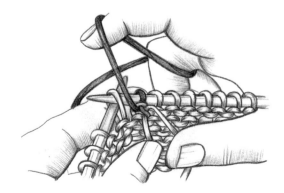

1 Lay the new colour (B) over the original colour (A). Twist the yarns over themselves and hold them in place.

2 Purl with the new colour (B).

Joining in a new colour in the middle of a row

When working in intarsia you will find yourself needing to join in a new colour in the middle of a row.

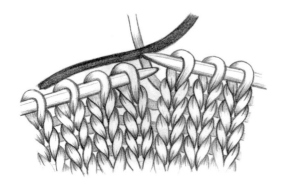

1. On a knit row, knit to the change in colour. Lay the new colour over the existing colour and between the two needles, with the tail to the left.

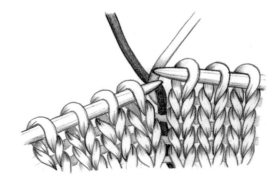

2. Bring the new colour under and then over the existing colour.

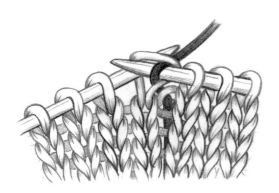

3. Knit the stitch with the new colour. Go back and pull gently on the tail to tighten up the first stitch in the new colour after you have knitted a couple more stitches.

Changing colours in a straight vertical line

Once you have joined in a new colour you may need to work for a number of rows changing these colours on both the knit rows and purl rows. This is often confusingly referred to as 'twisting' the yarns but it is a link rather than a twist. It is a common mistake to over-twist the yarns at this point and then the fabric will not lie flat.

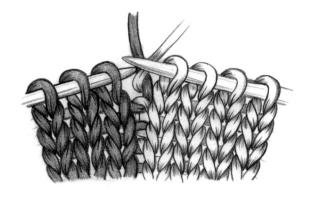

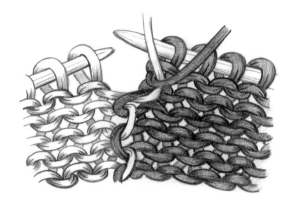

1 On a knit row, knit to the change in colour. Bring the new colour up from under the old colour and drop the old colour so that the new colour is ready to work with.

2 On a purl row, knit to the change in colour. Bring the new colour from the left under the old colour and up to the top. Drop the old colour and continue with the new colour.

Eliminating ends

If you are working a complex design it is always best to look for ways of eliminating ends so that you can cut down the number of hours that will be needed to sew them all in.

Look for shapes that perhaps have an outline, as with this diamond motif.

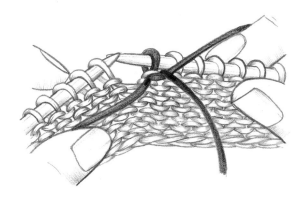

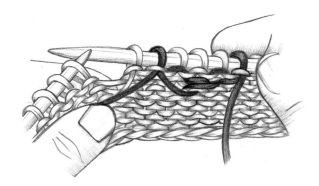

1 Take a length of the yarn required to work the whole motif and fold it in half. On the centre stitch of the motif, loop the fold over the right-hand needle.

2 On the next row, take one end of the yarn to the right and the other to the left, linking the outline and background colours on each row. If the motif is very small and the background colour remains the same, it is best to carry the background colour across the back of the motif, weaving it in if necessary.

Casting Off

There is one simple, most commonly used method of securing stitches once you have finished a piece of knitting – casting off. The cast-off edge should always have the same 'give' or elasticity as the fabric and you should always cast off in the stitch pattern used for the main fabric unless the pattern directs otherwise.

Knitwise

Knit two stitches. *Using the point of the left-hand needle, lift the first stitch on the right-hand needle over the second then drop it off the needle. Knit the next stitch and repeat from * until all stitches have been worked off the left-hand needle and only one stitch remains on the right-hand needle. Cut the yarn (leaving enough to sew in the end), thread the end through the stitch then slip it off the needle. Draw the yarn up firmly to fasten off.

Purlwise

Purl two stitches. *Using the point of the left-hand needle, lift the first stitch on the right-hand needle over the second and drop it off the needle. Purl the next stitch and repeat from * until all the stitches have been worked off the left-hand needle and only one stitch remains on the right-hand

needle. Secure the last stitch as described for casting off knitwise.

The excitement of arriving at the last stage of your knitting can make you cast off without the same care that you have used in the rest of the work. You should take into account the part of the garment you are working on. If it is a neckband, you need to make sure that your cast-off edge is not too tight, preventing the neck from going over the wearer's head. If you are a tight knitter, you may need to cast off with a larger needle. Most neckbands or frontbands on a jacket or cardigan are worked in rib and should be cast off 'ribwise' by knitting the knit stitches and purling the purl stitches as you cast off along the row. Lace stitches should also be cast off in pattern, slipping, making stitches or decreasing as you go to make sure that the fabric doesn't widen or gather up.

Tension (or gauge)

The correct tension (or gauge) is the most important contribution to the successful knitting of a garment. The information under this heading given at the beginning of all patterns refers to the number of stitches required to fill a particular area; for example, a frequent gauge indication would be '22 sts and 30 rows = 10cm (4in) square measured over stocking stitch on 4mm (size 6) needles'. This means that it is necessary to produce fabric made up of the proportion of stitches and rows as given in the tension paragraph in order to obtain the correct measurements for the garment you intend to knit, regardless of the needles you use. The needle size indicated in the pattern is the one which most knitters will use to achieve this tension, but it is the tension that is important, not needle size.

The way to ensure that you do achieve the correct tension is to work a tension sample or swatch before starting the main part of the knitting. Although this may seem to be time wasting and a nuisance, it can save the enormous amount of time and aggravation that would result from having knitted a garment the wrong size.

Tension Swatch

The instructions given in the tension paragraph of a knitting pattern are either for working in stocking stitch or in pattern stitch. If they are given in pattern stitch, it is necessary to work a multiple of stitches the same as the multiple required in the pattern. If in stocking stitch, any number can be cast on, but whichever method is used the swatch should always be at least 13cm (5in) wide. Work in pattern or stocking stitch according to the wording of the tension paragraph until the piece measures at least 10cm (4in) in depth. Break the yarn about 15cm (6in) from the work and thread this end through the stitches, then remove the knitting needle. Place

a pin vertically into the fabric a few stitches from the side edge. Measure 10cm (4in) carefully and insert a second pin. Count the stitches. If the number of stitches between the pins is fewer than specified in the pattern (even by half a stitch) your garment will be too large. Use smaller needles and knit another tension sample. If your sample has more stitches over 10cm (4in), the garment will be too small. Change to larger needles. Check the number of rows against the given tension also.

It is most important to get the width measurement correct before starting to knit. Length measurements can usually be adjusted during the course of the knitting by adjusting the measurements to underarm or sleeve length, which is frequently given as a measurement and not in rows.

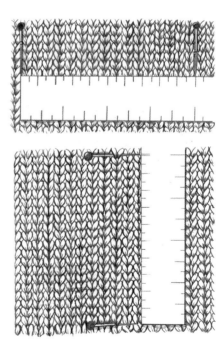

Following Charts

You should read a chart in the same way as you proceed with a piece of knitting: working from the bottom to the top. Each coloured block on the chart represents a stitch and each horizontal line a row (or part of a row, if the pattern is to be repeated across the whole width of the knitted piece).

Before starting to knit, take a good look at the chart to familiarize yourself with the pattern. When you have the right side of your work facing you, you need to follow the chart from right to left; when working on the reverse (wrong side), follow the chart from left to right. As you proceed, it may help you to keep track of where you are on the chart by placing a ruler above the line you are working.

Right-side rows are those where the right side of the fabric is facing you when you work, and wrong-side rows are those where the wrong side is facing you when you work. Row numbers are shown at the side of each chart, at the beginning of the row.

Pattern Repeats and Multiples

The 'multiple' or repeat of a pattern is given with each chart. For example, 'multiple of 6' means that you can cast on any number of stitches which is divisible by 6. This multiple is then repeated across the row the required number of times. In some charts, the pattern repeat is contained between heavier vertical lines. In some cases. there may be extra stitches at either end of a pattern repeat, which are edge stitches worked at the beginning and end of rows to complete the pattern and make the overall design symmetrical.

The simplest form of Fair Isle knitting is to repeat a single pattern over the entire width and depth of the fabric. A pattern band repeated many times becomes an all-over pattern; interesting effects can be also achieved by combining different pattern bands. As a general rule, it is best, when combining patterns, to choose those that have a similar number of stitches in their repeat.

As well as being repeated along the row, the number of rows in a pattern is also taken into consideration. Bands of patterns can vary from as little as one single row to 30 or more rows. Narrow bands, or 'peeries' have between one and seven rows and are generally used to separate larger bands. Border patterns are those with between 9 and 15 rows and are perfect for edgings or for all-over pattern repeats. Larger borders, with more than 15 rows, are generally based on 'OXO' designs – in other words, diamonds and crosses.

You will also see that there are a number of single star and snowflake motifs in this book. Like any of the other patterns, these can be repeated across a piece of knitted fabric; once again, take note of the number denoting the multiple or repeat, which is given with each chart.

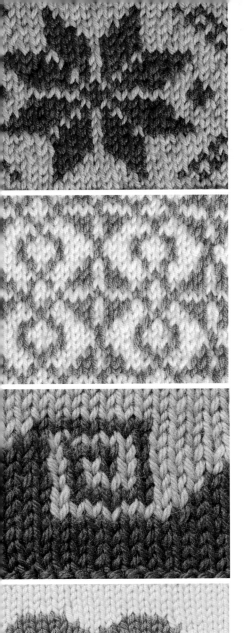

stitch
gallery

Little Dots (single)

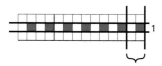

Rep 2 sts x 1 row

Little Dots (double)

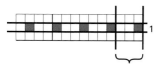

Rep 3 sts x 1 row

Short Dash

Rep 3 sts x 1 row

Dash

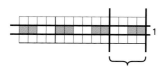

Rep 4 sts x 1 row

Dot and Dash

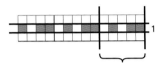

Rep 5 sts × 1 row

Long Dash

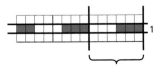

Rep 6 sts × 1 row

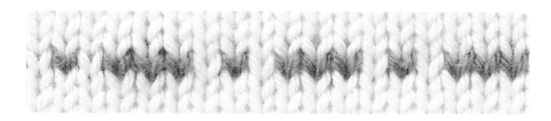

Dot and Long Dash

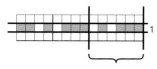

Rep 6 sts x 1 row

Small Zigzag

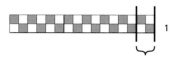

Rep 2 sts x 2 rows

Small Wave

Rep 3 sts × 2 rows

Back Stroke

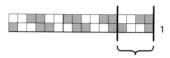

Rep 4 sts × 2 rows

Two-Wave

Rep 4 sts × 2 rows

Three-Wave

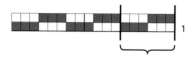

Rep 6 sts × 2 rows

Small Arch

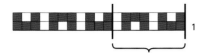

Rep 8 sts x 2 rows

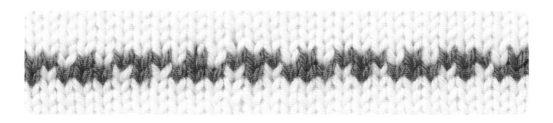

Triangle Wave 1

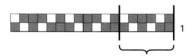

Rep 6 sts x 2 rows

Seeded Vertical Stripe

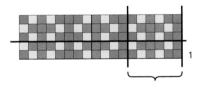

1

Rep 6 sts x 2 rows

Triangle and Square I

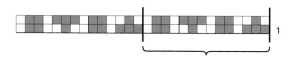

Rep 14 sts × 2 rows

Threaded Squares

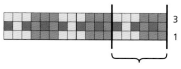

Rep 6 sts × 3 rows

Triangle and Square II

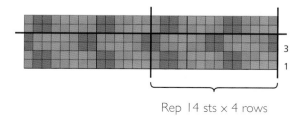

3

1

Rep 14 sts x 4 rows

Tall Blocks

Rep 3 sts × 3 rows

Post and Hook

Rep 3 sts × 3 rows

Broken Rows I

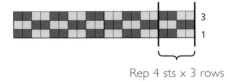

Rep 4 sts × 3 rows

Broken Rows II

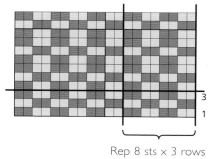

3

1

Rep 8 sts × 3 rows

High Tide

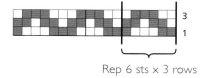

Rep 6 sts x 3 rows

Kirkwall Border

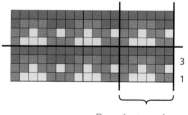

Rep 6 sts x 4 rows

Dancing Bears

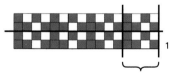

Rep 4 sts × 2 rows

Triangle Stacks

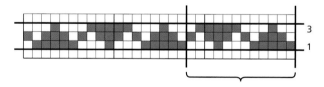

Rep 12 sts × 3 rows

Flotsam

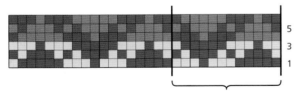

5
3
1

Rep 12 sts x 6 rows

Battlements (3-count)

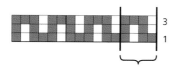

3
1

Rep 4 sts × 3 rows

Breakers

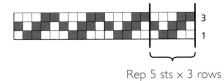

Rep 5 sts × 3 rows

Battlements (4-count) I

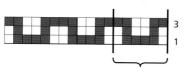

Rep 6 sts × 3 rows

Battlements (4-count) II

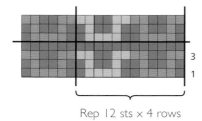

3

1

Rep 12 sts × 4 rows

Heather Peerie

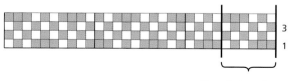

Rep 6 sts x 4 rows

Triangle and Dot

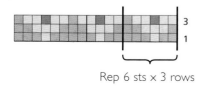

3

1

Rep 6 sts x 3 rows

Shoots and Seeds

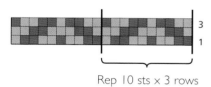

3

1

Rep 10 sts × 3 rows

Triangle Wave II

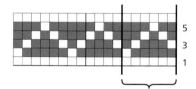

Rep 6 sts x 6 rows

Outline Triangle

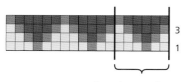

3

1

Rep 6 sts x 4 rows

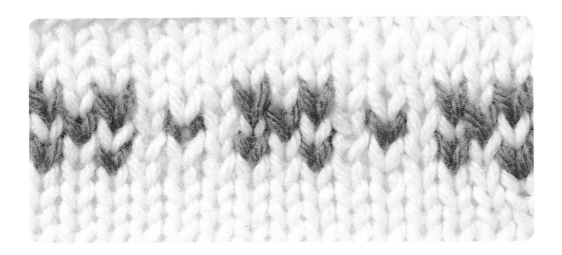

Five and One

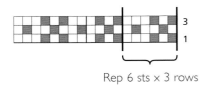

Rep 6 sts × 3 rows

Harvest Furrows

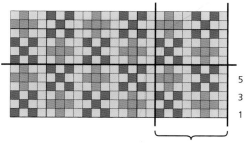

5
3
1

Rep 8 sts × 6 rows

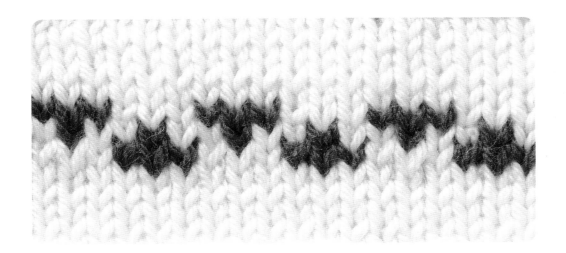

Triangle Wave III

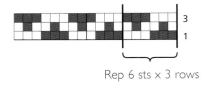

Rep 6 sts × 3 rows

Triangle Wave Border

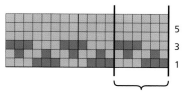

5
3
1

Rep 6 sts x 6 rows

H-border

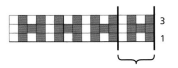

Rep 4 sts x 3 rows

Ploughed Furrows

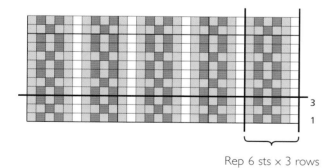

3
1

Rep 6 sts × 3 rows

Triangles and Strokes

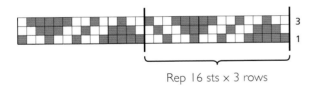

3
1

Rep 16 sts × 3 rows

Tree of Life

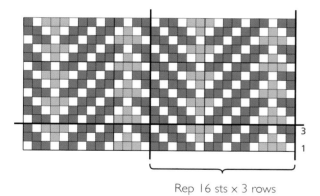

Rep 16 sts x 3 rows

Diagonal Lattice

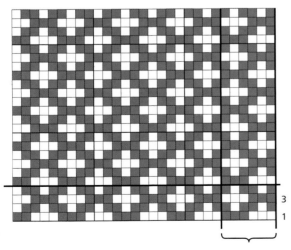

3

1

Rep 6 sts x 4 rows

Seeded Back Stroke

Rep 5 sts × 3 rows

Box and Dot

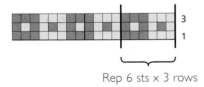

Rep 6 sts x 3 rows

Chequered Dot Border

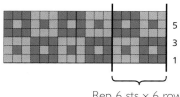

5
3
1

Rep 6 sts x 6 rows

Gull Wings

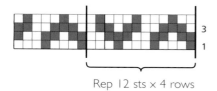

Rep 12 sts x 4 rows

Twinkling Diamonds

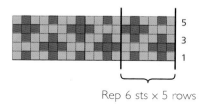

5
3
1

Rep 6 sts × 5 rows

Broken Crests

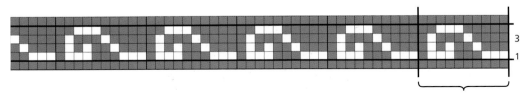

Rep 10 sts × 4 rows

3
1

Rocky Shore

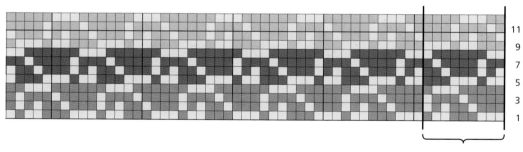

Rep 9 sts x 12 rows

Broken Zigzags

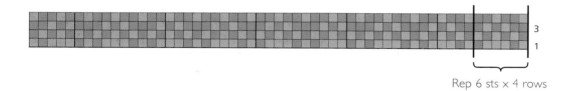

3

1

Rep 6 sts x 4 rows

Battlements (5-count)

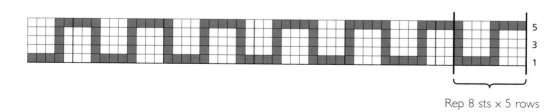

5
3
1

Rep 8 sts × 5 rows

Stormy Sea

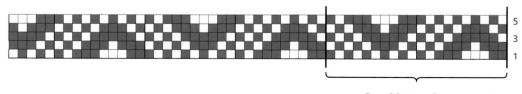

5
3
1

Rep 20 sts × 5 rows

Arrowhead Tweed Border

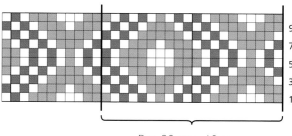

9
7
5
3
1

Rep 20 sts × 10 rows

Lattice Window I

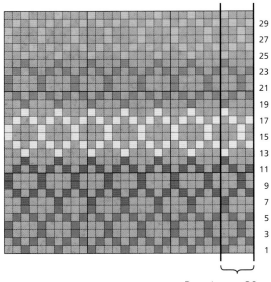

29
27
25
23
21
19
17
15
13
11
9
7
5
3
1

Rep 4 sts × 30 rows

Flight

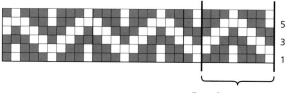

5
3
1

Rep 8 sts x 6 rows

Triangle Zigzag

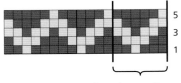

5
3
1

Rep 6 sts x 5 rows

Pretty Maids

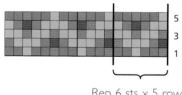

5

3

1

Rep 6 sts × 5 rows

Crossed Battlements

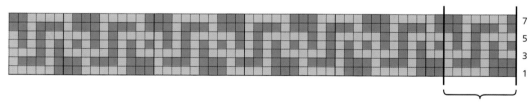

Rep 8 sts × 7 rows

Phlox

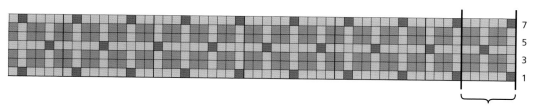

Rep 6 sts x 7 rows

Double-row Diamond

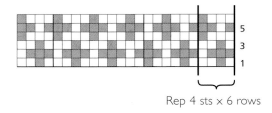

5

3

1

Rep 4 sts x 6 rows

Diamond Footpath

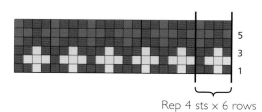

5
3
1

Rep 4 sts x 6 rows

Rose and Thistle

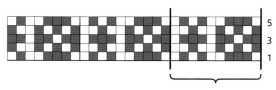

Rep 10 sts x 5 rows

Diamond Tweed Pattern

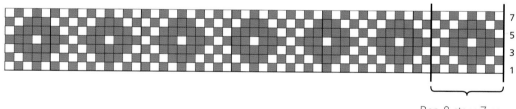

7
5
3
1

Rep 8 sts × 7 rows

Wave and Diamond Border

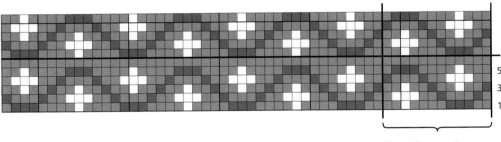

5
3
1

Rep 12 sts × 6 rows

Celtic Rose

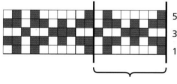

Rep 8 sts × 5 rows

Diamond Link and Dot

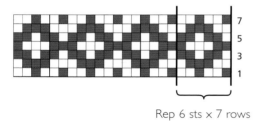

7
5
3
1

Rep 6 sts x 7 rows

Speckled Trellis

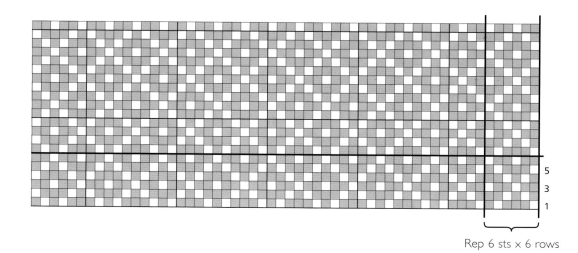

5
3
1

Rep 6 sts x 6 rows

Captive Diamond Border

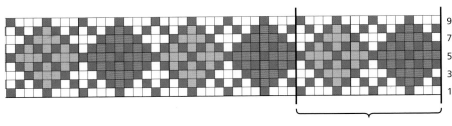

Rep 16 sts × 18 rows

Zigzag Fence

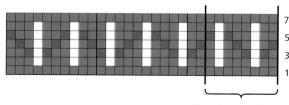

Rep 8 sts × 7 rows

Diamond Filigree

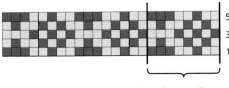

Rep 8 sts × 5 rows

Cabbages

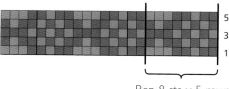

Rep 8 sts × 5 rows

Diamond Box Border

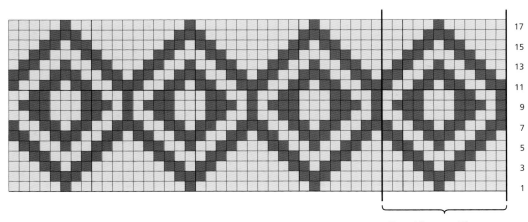

Rep 12 sts x 17 rows

17
15
13
11
9
7
5
3
1

Wandering Zigzag

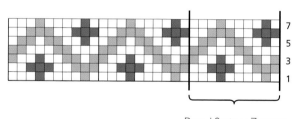

Rep 10 sts × 7 rows

Diamond and Cross Windowpane

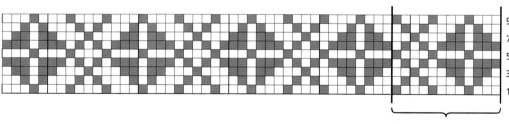

9
7
5
3
1

Rep 12 sts x 9 rows

Flower and Chalice

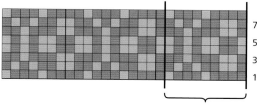

Rep 9 sts × 8 rows

Wall-walk

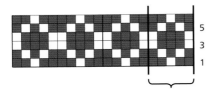

Rep 5 sts × 6 rows

Lattice Window II

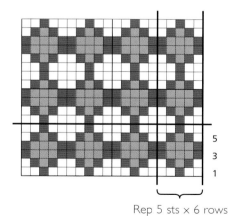

5
3
1

Rep 5 sts × 6 rows

Diamond and Cross

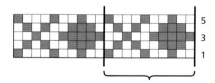

5
3
1

Rep 10 sts × 5 rows

Trellis with Blocks

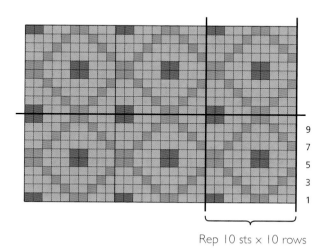

Rep 10 sts x 10 rows

Speckled Zigzag

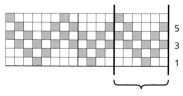

Rep 6 sts x 6 rows

Zigzag Tweed

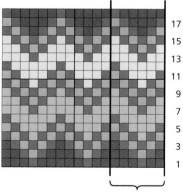

Rep 6 sts × 18 rows

Aubrieta

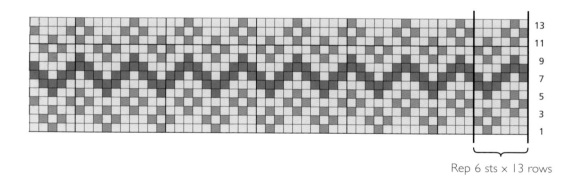

Rep 6 sts x 13 rows

Vertical Basketweave Lattice

7
5
3
1

Rep 30 sts x 8 rows

Arrowhead Zigzag

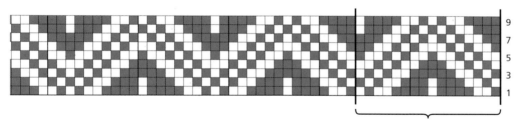

Rep 16 sts x 9 rows

Ripples Border

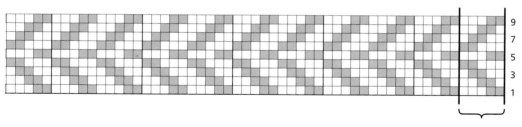

Rep 5 sts × 9 rows

Cosmea

13
11
9
7
5
3
1

Rep 16 sts × 13 rows

Diamond and Cross Windowpane II

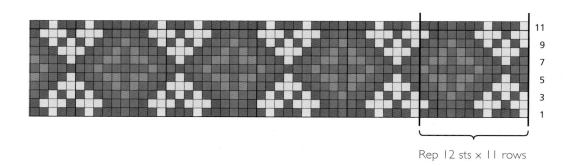

11
9
7
5
3
1

Rep 12 sts x 11 rows

Mosaic Path

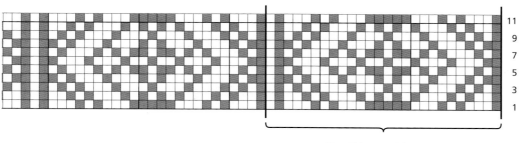

Rep 26 sts x 11 rows

Castle Window I

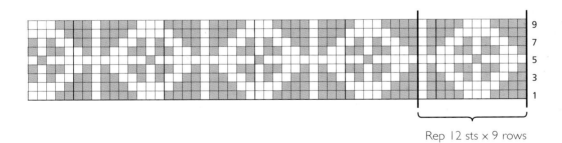

9
7
5
3
1

Rep 12 sts x 9 rows

Castle Window II

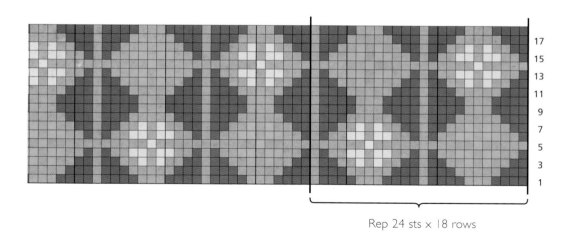

Rep 24 sts × 18 rows

17
15
13
11
9
7
5
3
1

Flora

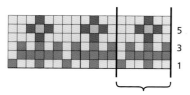

5
3
1

Rep 6 sts × 6 rows

Vertical Stripe I

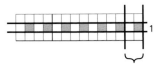

Rep 2 sts × 1 row

Line and Dot I

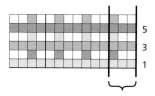

5

3

1

Rep 2 sts × 6 rows

Diamond Links

5
3
1

Rep 4 sts x 5 rows

Vertical Stripes II

Rep 3 sts x 1 row

Chain Link II

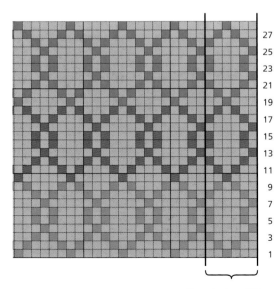

27
25
23
21
19
17
15
13
11
9
7
5
3
1

Rep 6 sts × 28 rows

Melissa

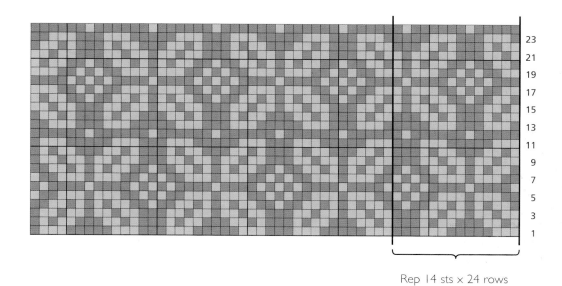

23
21
19
17
15
13
11
9
7
5
3
1

Rep 14 sts x 24 rows

Diamonds in the Snow

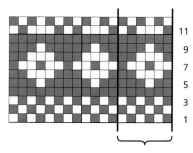

11
9
7
5
3
1

Rep 6 sts x 12 rows

Shuttered Windows

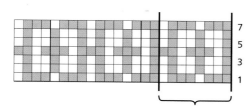

Rep 8 sts × 7 rows

Kirkwall

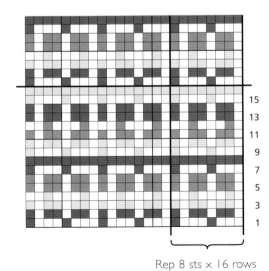

Rep 8 sts × 16 rows

15
13
11
9
7
5
3
1

Argyll Check

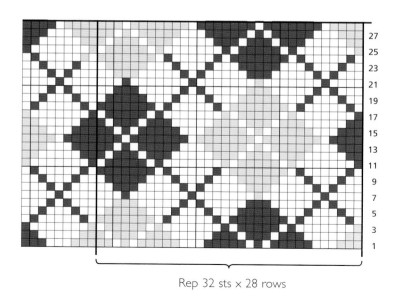

27
25
23
21
19
17
15
13
11
9
7
5
3
1

Rep 32 sts x 28 rows

Diamond Zigzag Bands

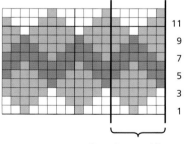

Rep 6 sts x 12 rows

Crossroads

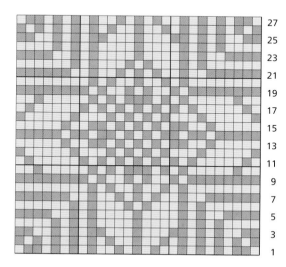

Rep 27 sts × 27 rows

Parterre

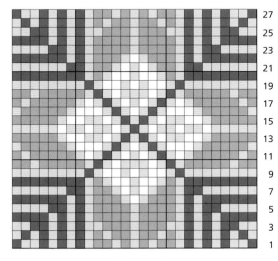

Rep 27 sts × 27 rows

Ladder of Hope

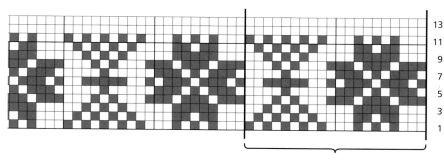

Rep 20 sts x 13 rows

Harbour Walls Motif

Rep 24 sts x 24 rows

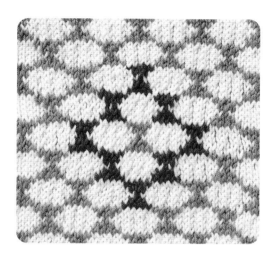

Berwick

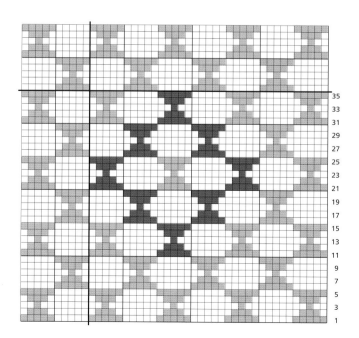

Rep 35 sts × 35 rows

Speckled Pinnacles

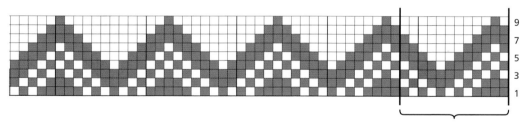

Rep 12 sts x 9 rows

9
7
5
3
1

Broken Zigzag Rows

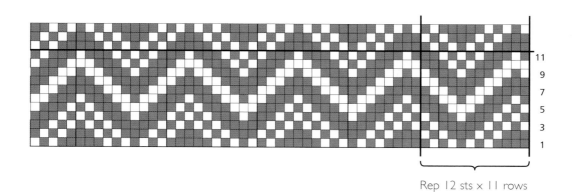

11
9
7
5
3
1

Rep 12 sts × 11 rows

Large Chain Link

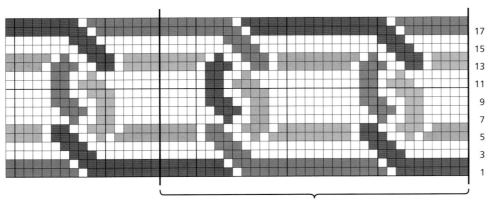

17
15
13
11
9
7
5
3
1

Rep 34 sts x 18 rows

Sprigged Snowflake Medallion

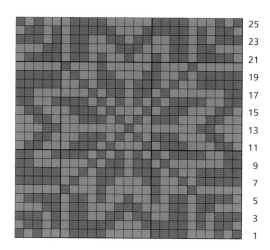

25
23
21
19
17
15
13
11
9
7
5
3
1

Rep 25 sts × 25 rows

Gallery Motif

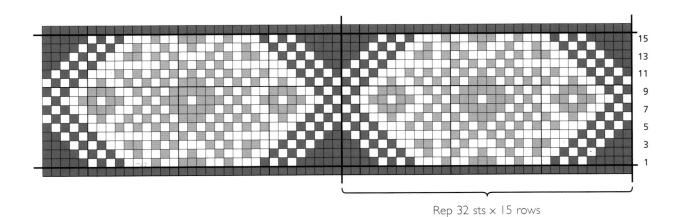

15
13
11
9
7
5
3
1

Rep 32 sts x 15 rows

Lillestrom Panel

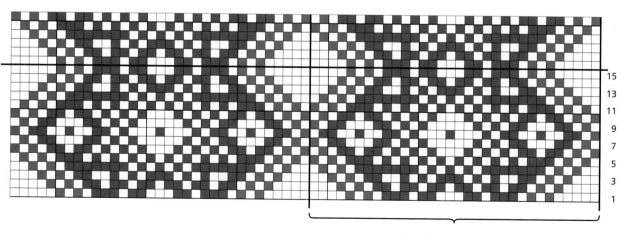

15
13
11
9
7
5
3
1

Rep 32 sts x 15 rows

Oslo Snowflake Motif

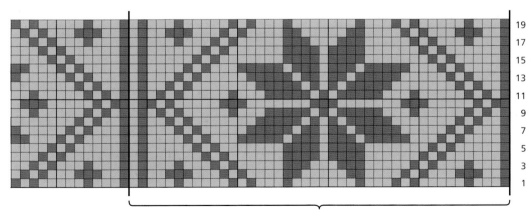

Rep 42 sts x 19 rows

19
17
15
13
11
9
7
5
3
1

Star and Arrow Lattice

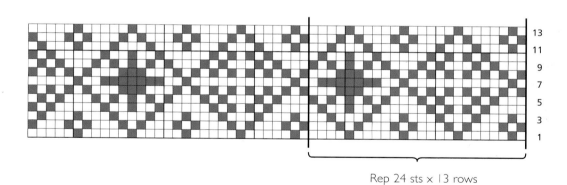

13
11
9
7
5
3
1

Rep 24 sts x 13 rows

Banded Lattice and Cross

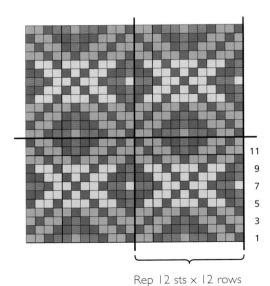

11
9
7
5
3
1

Rep 12 sts × 12 rows

Heraldic Border

Rep 14 sts x 11 rows

Flotilla

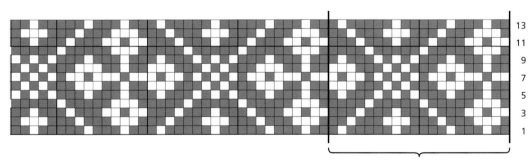

Rep 20 sts x 13 rows

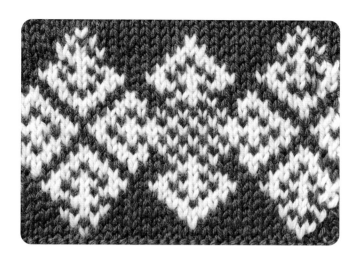

Trondheim Border

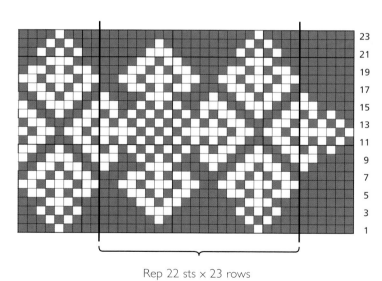

23
21
19
17
15
13
11
9
7
5
3
1

Rep 22 sts × 23 rows

Quadrant Cross

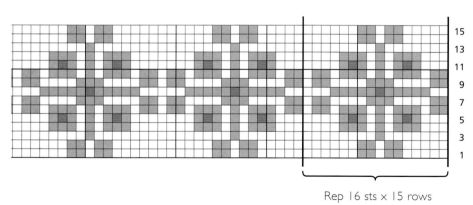

Rep 16 sts x 15 rows

North Cape 1

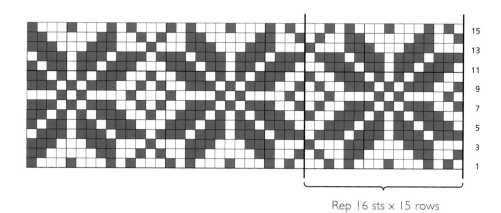

Rep 16 sts × 15 rows

North Cape II

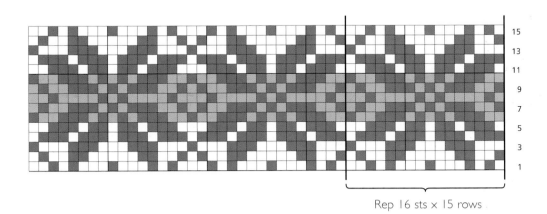

15
13
11
9
7
5
3
1

Rep 16 sts x 15 rows

Speckled Snowflake Medallion

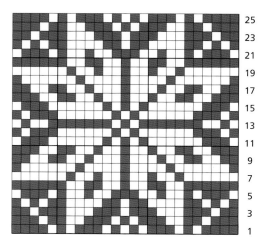

25
23
21
19
17
15
13
11
9
7
5
3
1

Rep 25 sts x 25 rows

Solid Snowflake

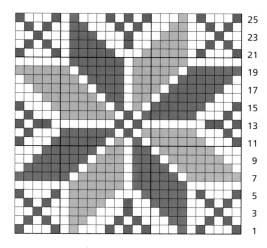

Rep 25 sts x 25 rows

Claymore

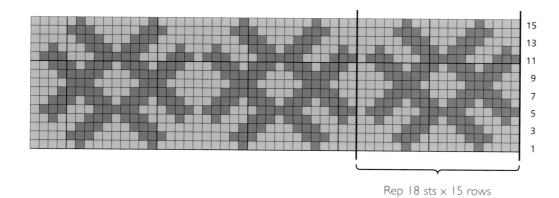

Rep 18 sts × 15 rows

St Nicholas Snowflake

31
29
27
25
23
21
19
17
15
13
11
9
7
5
3
1

Rep 31 sts x 31 rows

Norland Snowflake

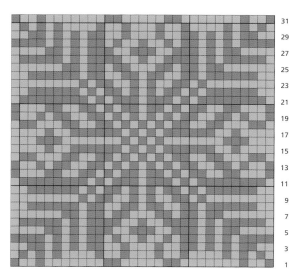

Rep 31 sts × 31 rows

Avenue

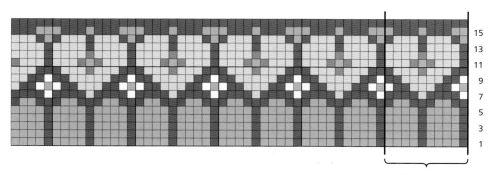

Rep 10 sts x 16 rows

Jacobean Flower Border

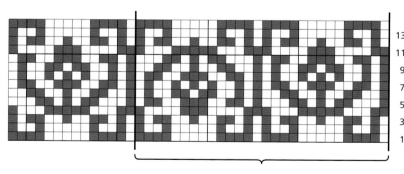

Rep 28 sts × 14 rows

Thistle and Ribbon

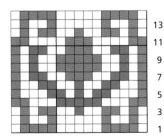

Rep 15 sts × 14 rows

Floret 1

35
33
31
29
27
25
23
21
19
17
15
13
11
9
7
5
3
1

Rep 33 sts × 35 rows

Floret 11

35
33
31
29
27
25
23
21
19
17
15
13
11
9
7
5
3
1

Rep 33 sts x 35 rows

Tromso Snowflake Panel

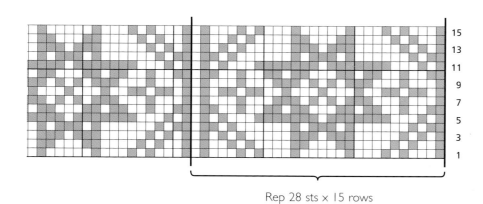

15
13
11
9
7
5
3
1

Rep 28 sts x 15 rows

Hydrangea Border

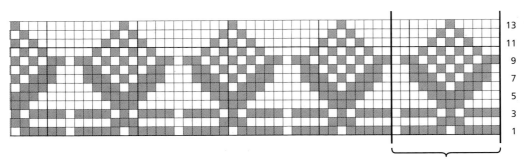

Rep 12 sts × 13 rows

13
11
9
7
5
3
1

Hydrangea Border II

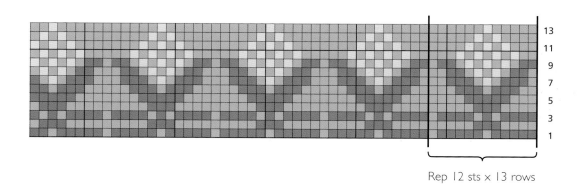

Rep 12 sts × 13 rows

13
11
9
7
5
3
1

Interlaced Tulips

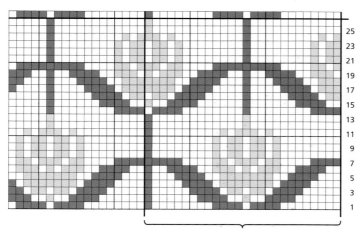

Rep 26 sts x 26 rows

Rambling Rose

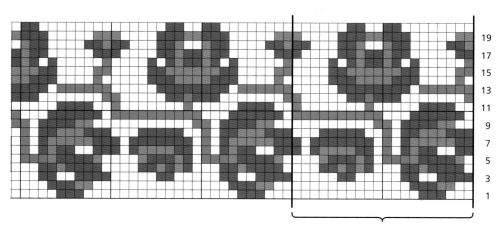

Rep 20 sts × 20 rows

19
17
15
13
11
9
7
5
3
1

Diamond Flower Border 1

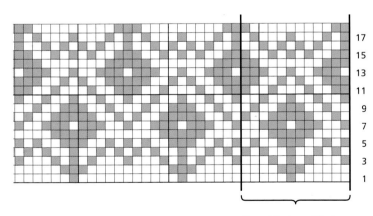

17
15
13
11
9
7
5
3
1

Rep 12 sts x 18 rows

Diamond Flower Border II

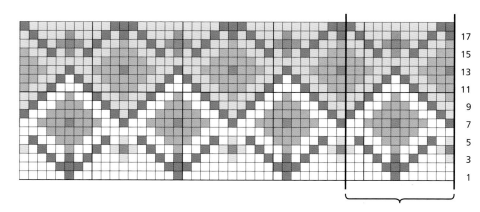

17
15
13
11
9
7
5
3
1

Rep 12 sts × 18 rows

Whirligig

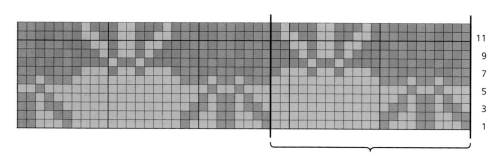

11
9
7
5
3
1

Rep 22 sts x 12 rows

Diamond and Snowflake Paths

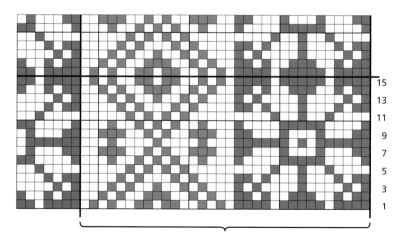

Rep 32 sts x 15 rows

Rose Crest

Rep 27 sts × 27 rows

Winter Rose Medallion

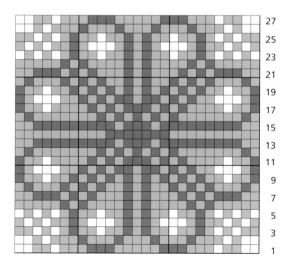

Rep 27 sts x 27 rows

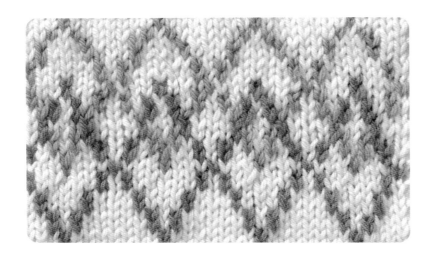

Dancing Diamonds

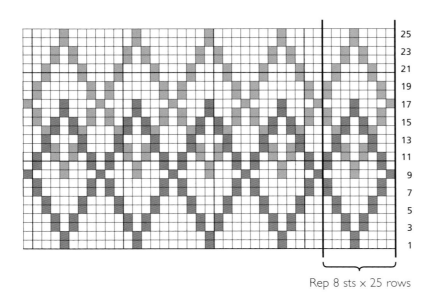

Rep 8 sts x 25 rows

Multiple Stripes

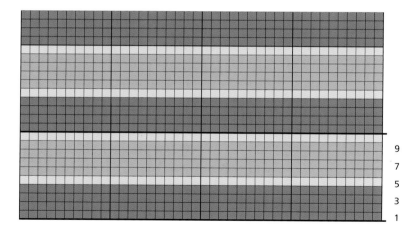

Rep 1 st × 10 rows

Diamond and Lozenge Tweed Border

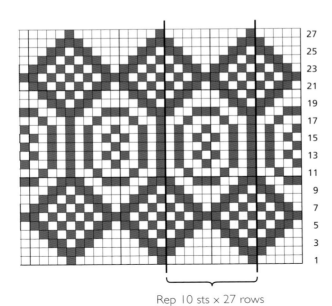

27
25
23
21
19
17
15
13
11
9
7
5
3
1

Rep 10 sts × 27 rows

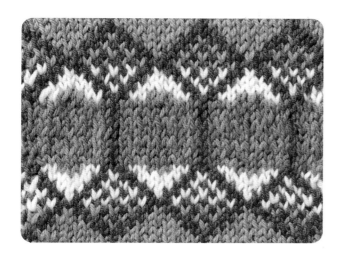

Diamond and Lozenge Banded Border

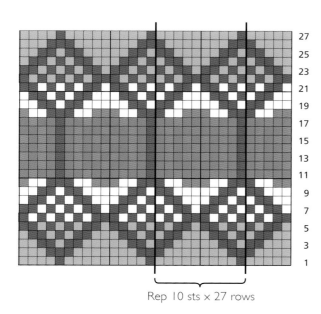

27
25
23
21
19
17
15
13
11
9
7
5
3
1

Rep 10 sts × 27 rows

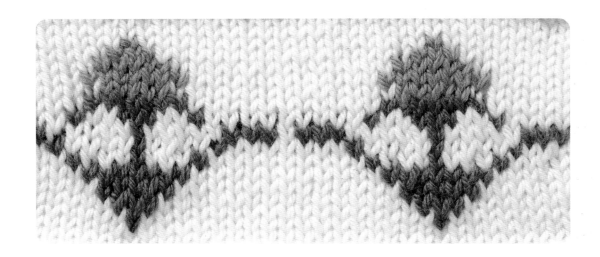

Scottish Thistles 1

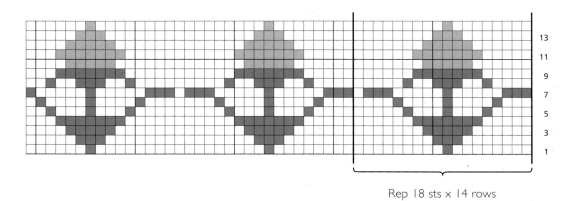

Rep 18 sts x 14 rows

13
11
9
7
5
3
1

Scottish Thistles II

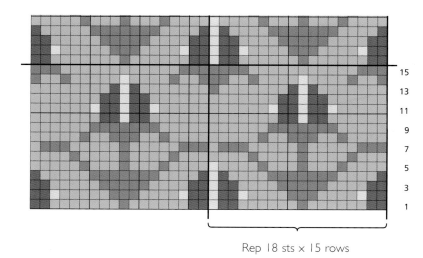

Rep 18 sts × 15 rows

15
13
11
9
7
5
3
1

Cairn

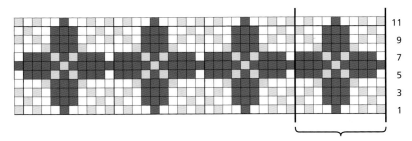

11
9
7
5
3
1

Rep 10 sts × 11 rows

Sheild and Cross

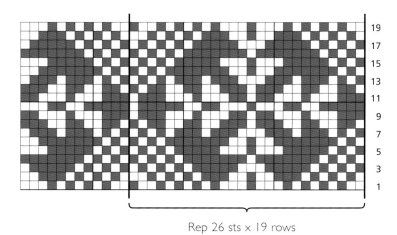

Rep 26 sts x 19 rows

Little Minch

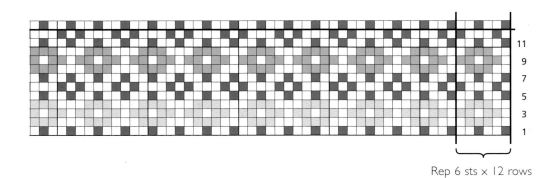

11
9
7
5
3
1

Rep 6 sts x 12 rows

Grandma's Garden

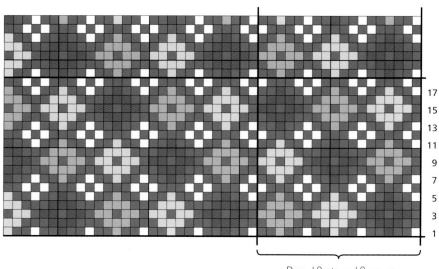

17
15
13
11
9
7
5
3
1

Rep 18 sts × 18 rows

Quatrefoil

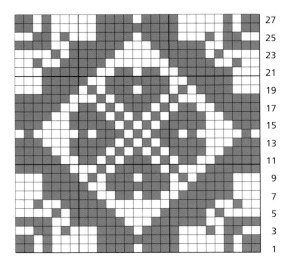

Rep 27 sts × 27 rows

Argyll Diamond Motif

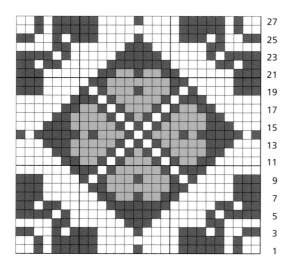

Rep 27 sts × 27 rows

Hellenic Wave

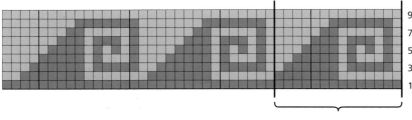

Rep 14 sts x 9 rows

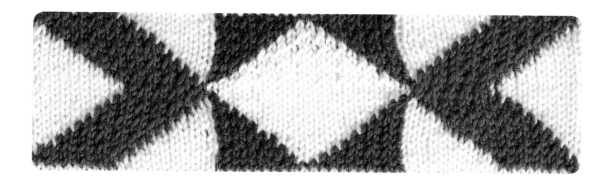

Algorithm

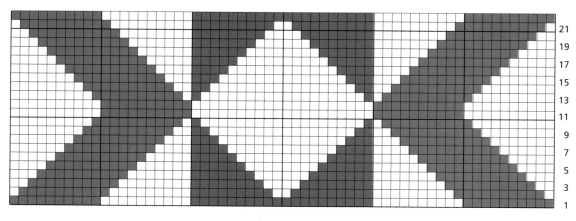

Rep 60 sts x 22 rows

Diathus and Pannier Border

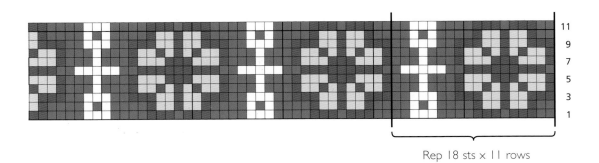

Rep 18 sts × 11 rows

Campion and Pannier Border

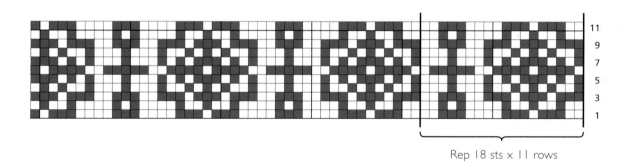

Rep 18 sts x 11 rows

Herbaceous Border

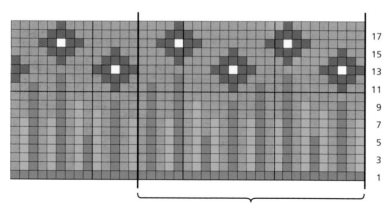

Rep 25 sts × 18 rows

Large Vertical Stripe

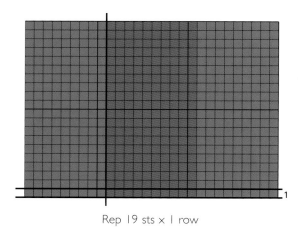

Rep 19 sts × 1 row

Even Stripes

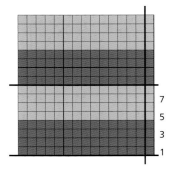

Rep 1 st x 8 rows

Uneven Stripes

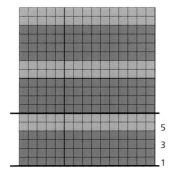

5
3
1

Rep 1 st × 6 rows

Michaelmas

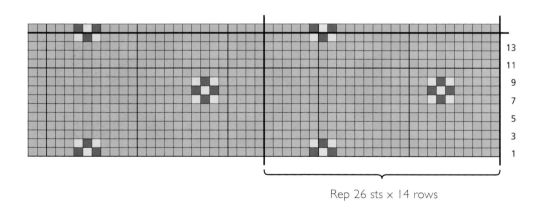

13
11
9
7
5
3
1

Rep 26 sts × 14 rows

Stepping Stones

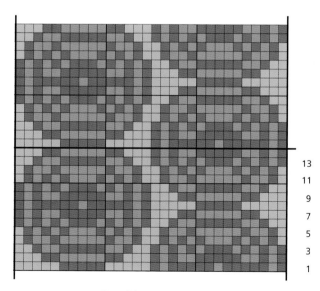

13
11
9
7
5
3
1

Rep 30 sts × 14 rows

Lads and Lasses I

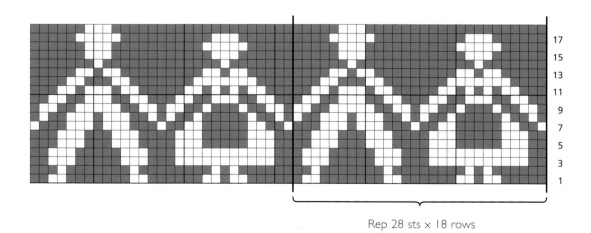

17
15
13
11
9
7
5
3
1

Rep 28 sts × 18 rows

Lads and Lasses II

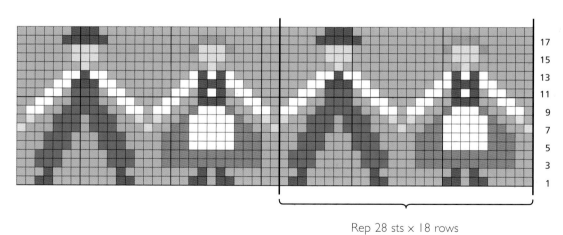

Rep 28 sts × 18 rows

Framed Heart Motif

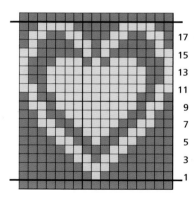

Rep 17 sts x 18 rows

Christmas Lights

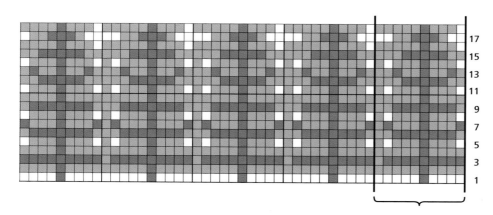

17
15
13
11
9
7
5
3
1

Rep 10 sts x 18 rows

Acrobats

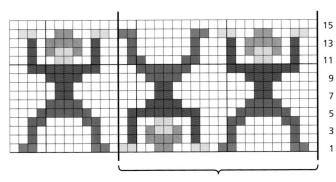

Rep 22 sts x 15 rows

Dancing Ballerinas

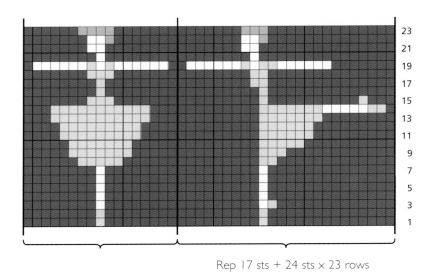

Rep 17 sts + 24 sts × 23 rows

Belladonna

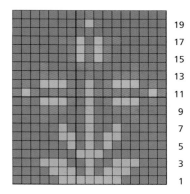

Rep 17 sts × 20 rows

Campion

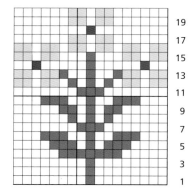

Rep 17sts x 20 rows

Standard Flower

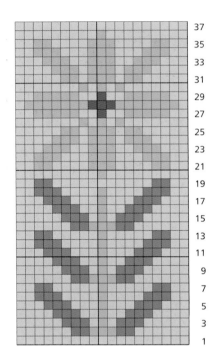

Rep 19 sts × 37 rows

Foxglove

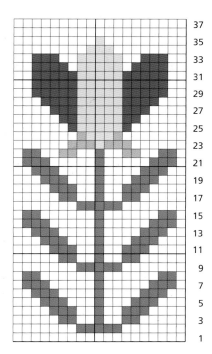

Rep 19 sts x 37 rows

Juniper

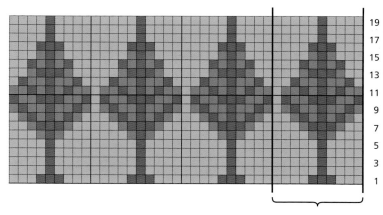

19
17
15
13
11
9
7
5
3
1

Rep 10 sts x 19 rows

Pansy Trio

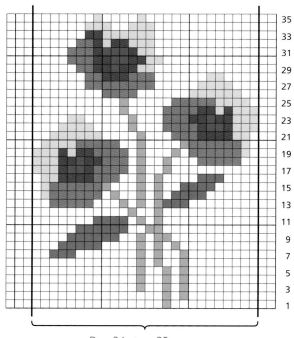

Rep 26 sts × 35 rows

Solid Heart

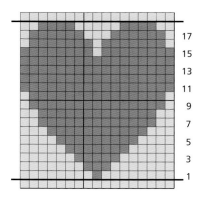

17
15
13
11
9
7
5
3
1

Rep 17 sts × 18 rows

Dancing Ladies

Rep 35 sts × 32 rows

Saxifrage

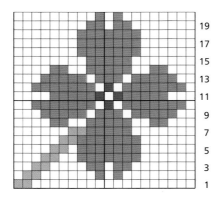

Rep 20 sts x 20 rows

Single Bud

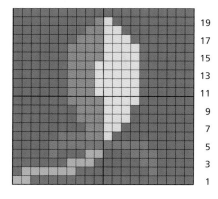

Rep 20 sts × 20 rows

Cranesbill

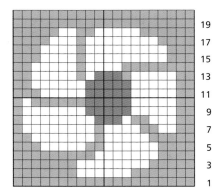

Rep 20 sts x 20 rows

Magnolia

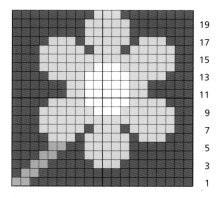

Rep 20 sts x 20 rows

19
17
15
13
11
9
7
5
3
1

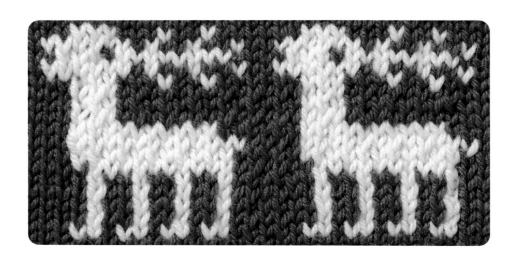

Marching Reindeer

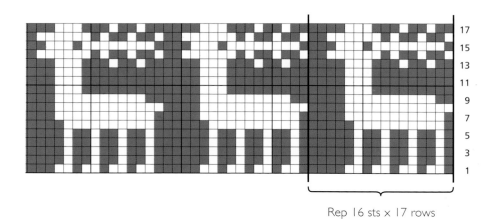

17
15
13
11
9
7
5
3
1

Rep 16 sts x 17 rows

Large Tulip

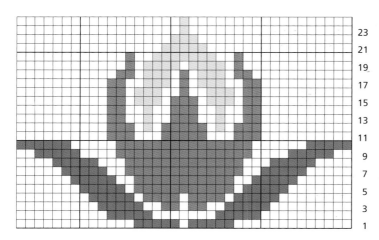

Rep 37 sts x 24 rows

Butterflies

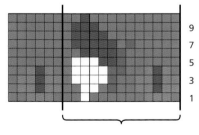

Rep 13 sts x 10 rows

Pig

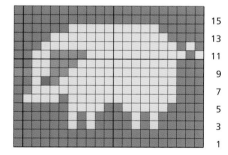

											15
											13
											11
											9
											7
											5
											3
											1

Rep 21 sts x 16 rows

Horse

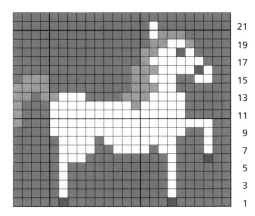

Rep 24 sts × 22 rows

Playful Kitten

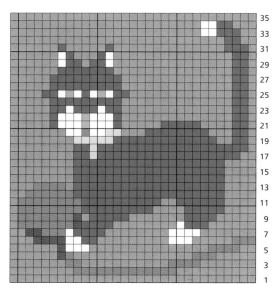

Rep 31 sts × 35 rows

Musical Notes

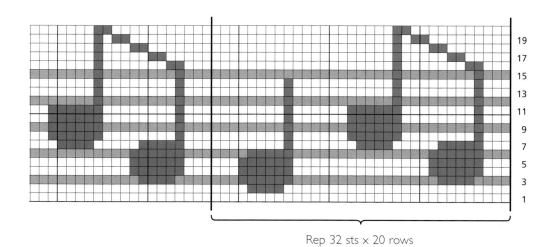

Rep 32 sts × 20 rows

Balloon

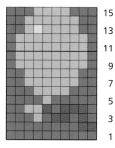

15
13
11
9
7
5
3
1

Rep 10 sts × 15 rows

Snowman

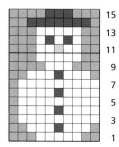

Rep 10 sts x 15 rows

Rocket

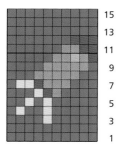

15
13
11
9
7
5
3
1

Rep 10 sts × 15 rows

Little House

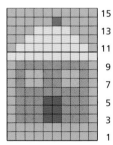

Rep 10 sts × 15 rows

Key

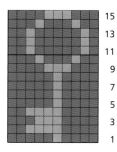

15
13
11
9
7
5
3
1

Rep 10 sts × 15 rows

Umbrella

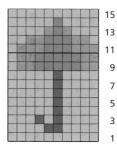

Rep 10 sts x 15 rows

Anchor

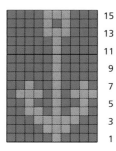

Rep 10 sts × 15 rows

Rabbit

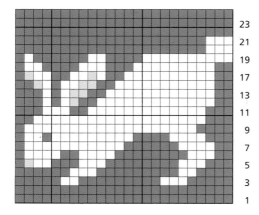

Rep 24 sts × 22 rows

A

B

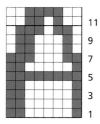

Rep 8 sts × 12 rows

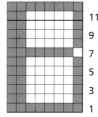

Rep 8 sts × 12 rows

C

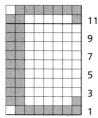

11
9
7
5
3
1

Rep 8 sts × 12 rows

D

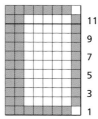

11
9
7
5
3
1

Rep 8 sts × 12 rows

E

F

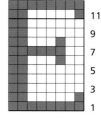

Rep 8 sts × 12 rows

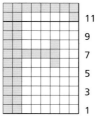

Rep 8 sts × 12 rows

G

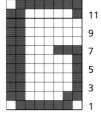

11
9
7
5
3
1

Rep 8 sts × 12 rows

H

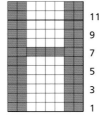

11
9
7
5
3
1

Rep 8 sts × 12 rows

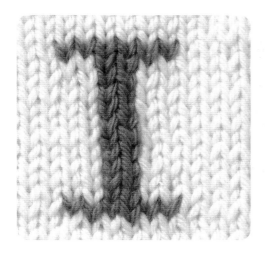

I

J

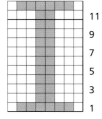

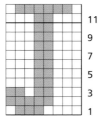

Rep 8 sts × 12 rows

Rep 8 sts × 12 rows

K

L

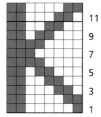

11
9
7
5
3
1

Rep 8 sts × 12 rows

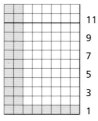

11
9
7
5
3
1

Rep 8 sts × 12 rows

M

N

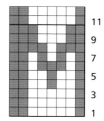

Rep 8 sts x 12 rows

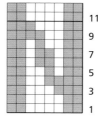

Rep 8 sts x 12 rows

O

P

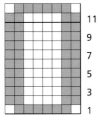

11
9
7
5
3
1

Rep 8 sts × 12 rows

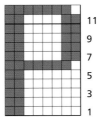

11
9
7
5
3
1

Rep 8 sts × 12 rows

Q

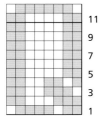

Rep 8 sts × 12 rows

R

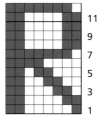

Rep 8 sts × 12 rows

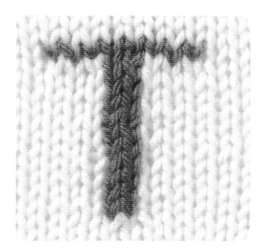

S

T

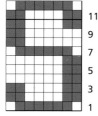

Rep 8 sts × 12 rows

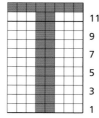

Rep 8 sts × 12 rows

U

V

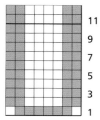

Rep 8 sts × 12 rows

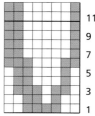

Rep 8 sts × 12 rows

W

X

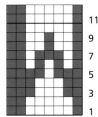

Rep 8 sts x 12 rows

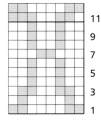

Rep 8 sts x 12 rows

Y

Z

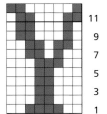

Rep 8 sts × 12 rows

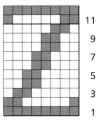

Rep 8 sts × 12 rows

a

b

Rep 6 sts × 9 rows

Rep 6 sts × 9 rows

c

d

Rep 6 sts × 9 rows

Rep 6 sts × 9 rows

e

f

Rep 6 sts × 9 rows

Rep 6 sts × 9 rows

g

h

Rep 6 sts × 9 rows

Rep 6 sts × 9 rows

i
_____

j
_____

Rep 6 sts x 9 rows

Rep 6 sts x 9 rows

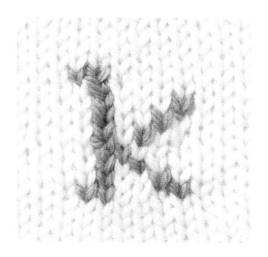

k

l

Rep 6 sts x 9 rows

Rep 6 sts x 9 rows

m

n

Rep 6 sts x 9 rows

Rep 6 sts x 9 rows

o

p

Rep 6 sts × 9 rows

Rep 6 sts × 9 rows

q
_____

r
_____

Rep 6 sts × 9 rows

Rep 6 sts × 9 rows

s

t

Rep 6 sts x 9 rows

Rep 6 sts x 9 rows

u

Rep 6 sts × 9 rows

v

Rep 6 sts × 9 rows

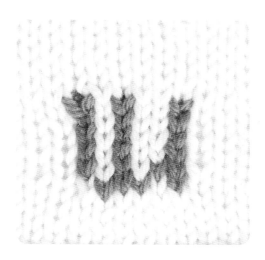

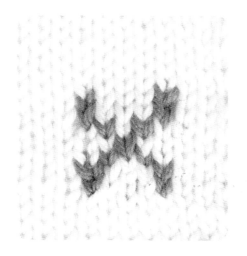

W

X

Rep 6 sts x 9 rows

Rep 6 sts x 9 rows

y
_____

z
_____

9
7
5
3
1

Rep 6 sts × 9 rows

9
7
5
3
1

Rep 6 sts × 9 rows

1

2

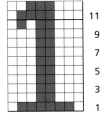

11

9

7

5

3

1

Rep 8 sts × 12 rows

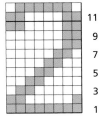

11

9

7

5

3

1

Rep 8 sts × 12 rows

3

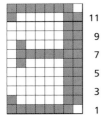

11
9
7
5
3
1

Rep 8 sts × 12 rows

4

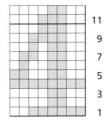

11
9
7
5
3
1

Rep 8 sts × 12 rows

5

6

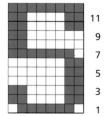

Rep 8 sts × 12 rows

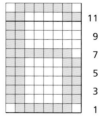

Rep 8 sts × 12 rows

7

8

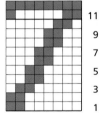

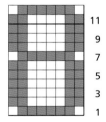

11

9

7

5

3

1

11

9

7

5

3

1

Rep 8 sts × 12 rows

Rep 8 sts × 12 rows

9

0

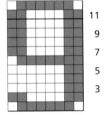

11
9
7
5
3

Rep 8 sts × 12 rows

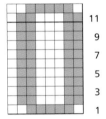

11
9
7
5
3
1

Rep 8 sts × 12 rows

index

0 267
1 263
2 263
3 264
4 264
5 265
6 265
7 266
8 266
9 267

A 237
a 250
Acrobats 208
Algorithm 195
Anchor 235
Argyll Check 133
Argyll Diamond Motif 193
Arrowhead Tweed Border 77
Arrowhead Weave 112
Aubrieta 110
Avenue 166

B 237
b 250
Back Stroke 30
Balloon 229
Banded Lattice and Cross 150
Bannock Trellis Pattern 78
Battlements (3-count) 49
Battlements (4-count) I 51
Battlements (4-count) II 52
Battlements (5-count) 75
Belladona 210
Berwick 139
Box and Dot 68
Breakers 50
Broken Crests 72
Broken Fence 38
Broken Rows I 40
Broken Rows II 41
Broken Zigzag Rows 141

Broken Zigzags 74
Butterflies 224

C 238
c 251
Cabbages 99
Cairn 188
Campion 211
Campion and Pannier Border 197
Captive Diamond Border 96
Castle Window I 117
Castle Window II 118
Celtic Rose 93
Chain Link I 127
Chain Link II 128
Chequered Dot Border 69
Christmas Lights 207
Claymore 159
Cosmea 114
Country Lanes 124
Cranesbill 220
Crossed Battlements 86
Crossroads 135

D 238
d 251
Dancing Ballerinas 209
Dancing Bears 46
Dancing Diamonds 182
Dancing Ladies 217
Dash 27
Diagonal Lattice 66
Diamond and Cross 106
Diamond and Cross
    Windowpane 102
Diamond and Cross
    Windowpane II 115
Diamond and Lozenge Banded
    Border 185
Diamond and Lozenge Tweed
    Border 184

Diamond and Snowflake Paths
    179
Diamond Box Border 100
Diamond Filigree 98
Diamond Flower Border I 176
Diamond Flower Border II 177
Diamond Footpath 89
Diamond Link and Dot 94
Diamond Tweed Pattern 91
Diamond Zigzag Bands 134
Diamonds in the Snow 130
Diamonds Links 122
Diathus and Pannier Border
    196
Dot and Dash 28
Dot and Long Dash 29
Double Vertical Stripes 126
Double-row Diamond 88

E 239
e 252
Even Stripes 200

F 239
f 252
Fish Hooks 145
Five and One 58
Flight 83
Flora 119
Floret I 169
Floret II 170
Flotilla 152
Flotsam 48
Flower and Chalice 103
Foxglove 213
Framed Heart Motif 206

G 240
g 253
Gallery Motif 146
Grandma's Garden 191
Gull Wings 70

H 240
h 253
Harbour Walls Motif 138
Harvest Furrows 59
H-Border 62
Heather Peerie 53
Hellenic Wave 194
Heraldic Border 151
Herbaceous Border 198
High Tide 44
Horse 226
Hydrangea Border 172
Hydrangea Border II 173

I 241
i 254
Interlaced Tulips 174

J 241
j 254
Jacobean Flower Border 167
Juniper 214

K 242
k 255
Key 233
Kirkwall 132
Kirkwall Border 45

L 242
l 255
Ladder of Hope 137
Lads and Lasses 204
Lads and Lasses II 205
Large Chain Link 142
Large Tulip 223
Large Vertical Stripe 199
Lattice Heart Border 144
Lattice Window I 82
Lattice Window II 105
Lillestrom Panel 147
Line and Dot I 121

resources

Rowan
Green Lane Mill
Holmfirth
HD9 2DX
England
www.knitrowan.com
+44 (0)1484 681881

Publisher's Acknowledgements
First and foremost, we'd like to thank Rowan Yarns for suppplying the yarns used in this book. We would like to thank all those who helped recreate the swatches: Melina Kalatzi, Sarah Hazell, Carole Downie, Cathy MacDonald, Jenny McHardy, Rosalind Campbell and Annette Travers. Lastly, we would like to thank all editors, past and present, who have contributed to the series. Photography by Geoff Dann.

Other titles currently available in the Harmony Guides series:

KNIT

CROCHET

Love crafts?
Crafters, keep updated on al exciting news from Collins & Brown. Email lovecrafts@anovabooks.com to register for free email alerts and author events.

Line and Dot II 125
Little Dots (double) 26
Little Dots (single) 26
Little House 232
Little Minch 190
Long Dash 28

M 243
m 256
Magnolia 221
Marching Reindeer 222
Melissa 129
Michaelmas 202
Minerva 161
Mosaic Path 116
Multiple Stripes 183
Musical Notes 228

N 243
n 256
Norland Snowflake 165
North Cape I 155
North Cape II 156

O 244
o 257
Oslo Snowflake Motif 148
Outline Triangle 57

P 244
p 257
Pansy Trio 215
Parterre 136
Phlox 87
Pig 225
Playful Kitten 227
Ploughed Furrows 63
Post and Hook 37
Pretty Maids 85

Q 245
q 258

Quadrant Cross 154
Quatrefoil 192

R 245
r 258
Rabbit 236
Rambling Rose 175
Ripples Border 113
Rocket 231
Rocky Shore 73
Rose and Thistle 90
Rose Crest 180

S 246
s 259
Saxifrage 218
Scottish Thistles I 186
Scottish Thistles II 187
Seeded Back Stroke 67
Seeded Vertical Stripe 33
Shield and Cross 189
Ship in Full Sail 160
Shoots and Seeds 55
Short Dash 27
Shuttered Windows 131
Single Bud 219
Single Fence 39
Small Arch 32
Small Arrowhead 42
Small Wave 30
Small Zigzag 29
Snowman 230
Solid Heart 216
Solid Snowflake 158
Speckled Fence 43
Speckled Pinnacles 140
Speckled Snowflake Medallion
    157
Speckled Trellis 95
Speckled Zigzag 108
Sprigged Snowflake Medallion
    143

St Nicholas Snowflake 164
Standard Flower 212
Star and Arrow Lattice 149
Stepping Stones 203
Stormy Sea 76

T 246
t 259
Tall Blocks 36
Thistle and Ribbon 168
Threaded Squares 34
Three-Wave 31
Tree of Life 65
Trellis with Blocks 107
Triangle and Dot 54
Triangle and Square I 34
Triangle and Square II 34
Triangle Stacks 47
Triangle Wave Border 61
Triangle Wave I 32
Triangle Wave II 56
Triangle Wave III 60
Triangle Zigzag 84
Triangles and Strokes 64
Tromso Snowflake 163
Tromso Snowflake Panel 171
Trondheim Border 153
Tulip Wave 79
Twinkling Diamonds 71
Two Tribes 162
Two-Wave 31

U 247
u 260
Umbrella 234
Uneven Stripes 201

V 247
v 260
Vertical Basketweave Lattice 111
Vertical Stripe I 120
Vertical Stripes II 123

W 248
w 261
Wall-Walk 104
Wandering Zigzag 101
Wave and Diamond Border 92
Wave Crest I 80
Wave Crest II 81
Whirligig 178
Winter Rose Medallion 181

X 248
x 261

Y 249
y 262

Z 249
z 262
Zigzag Fence 97
Zigzag Tweed 109